Stay Posted!

Quickie Stickies

100
Pick-Me-Ups
for When You're
Feeling
Unglued

by Karen Salmansohn

illustrated by Ellen Weinstein

WORKMAN PUBLISHING   NEW YORK

Library of Congress Cataloging-in-Publication Data
Salmansohn, Karen.
Quickie stickies: 100 pick-me-ups for when you're feeling unglued /
written by Karen Salmansohn ; illustrated by Ellen Weinstein.
p. cm.
ISBN 0-7611-2895-6
1. Affirmations. I. Weinstein, Ellen. II. Title.

BF697.5.S47S35 2003
158.1--dc21   2002041176

Thanks to cover model Lucia Davis
and cover photographer Josh Gosfield.

Workman books are available at special discounts when purchased
in bulk for premiums and sales promotions as well as for fund-raising
or educational use. Special editions or book excerpts can also be
created to specification. For details, contact the Special Sales
Director at the address below.

WORKMAN PUBLISHING COMPANY, INC.
708 Broadway
New York, NY 10003-9555
www.workman.com

Printed in China

First printing April 2003
10 9 8 7 6 5 4 3 2 1

INTRODUCTION

I once had this boyfriend (Josh) whom I spoiled silly with notes I'd stick in surprising places for him to find. For instance, I'd stick a sexy/romantic note on his plastic-wrapped tuna sandwich, so when he opened it he'd be hungry for more than lunch. Or I'd post an inspirational note on the bathroom mirror for him to see before he went running—to psych him up for those hills! Or I'd stick an encouraging note in his schedule book on a day that I knew he had a difficult meeting. Anyway, Josh loved these notes so much that I became inspired to write them for others as well—friends, co-workers, family members . . . myself, YOU! Here's how it works: You can read this book straight through like a regular book, and if you see a particular page that speaks to you, simply peel it out with a gentle tug and stick it up anywhere it will inspire you or a friend or co-worker—a computer, refrigerator, steering wheel, office coffee pot, etc. It's your choice how you pick 'em and where you stick 'em. There's only one goal: that these assorted Stickies will help to give your moods a big, powerful lift!

If you're **not living** on the **edge**, you're taking **up** too much **room**.

Willpower beats **Shouldpower**
every time!

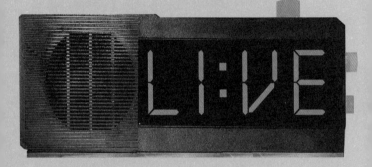

The only thing a gal can ever **change** in her man is maybe his **wardrobe**.

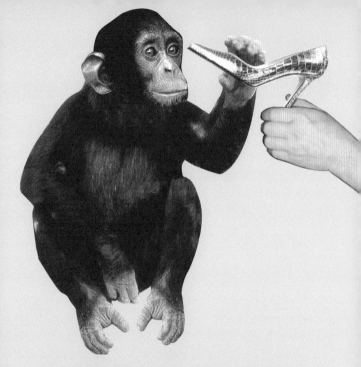

Stop looking for bananas from people who have no bananas. Some people just cannot offer you what you **need.**

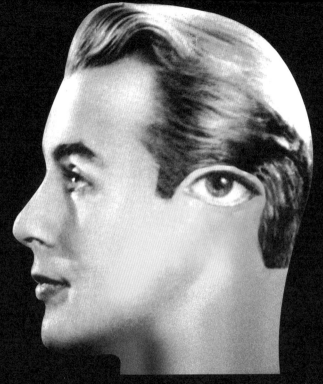

To **hear** better, use your **eyes**.
(83% of sensory communication is seen, not heard.)

I am so
proactive,
I am
preactive.

Positive **thoughts** attract positive **outcomes**
...just as **like** attracts **like**
love attracts **love**
and **velvet** attracts **cat hair**

Taking **no action** is also **an action.**

SHUT UP
and meditate.

FEAR OF COMMITMENT:
it could happen to you or someone
you can't love.

WARNING: OBJECTS IN MIRROR WILL APPEAR LARGER DURING PMS

↑
rear view mirror

I'm on a **no-nuts diet. No** nutty people are allowed in my **life**.

Is money worth the price?

MONDAY	16
TUESDAY	17
SOMEDAY	18
WEDNESDAY	19
THURSDAY	20
FRIDAY	21
SATURDAY	22
SUNDAY	23

Someday is **not** a day of the week.

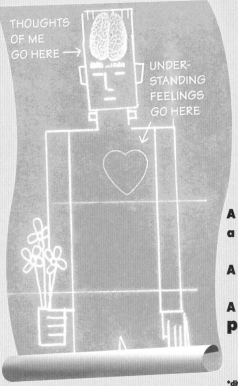

THOUGHTS OF ME GO HERE →

UNDER-STANDING FEELINGS GO HERE

A **man** is not a **project.***

A man is a **man.**

A project is a **project.**

*ditto for a woman

THE GOOD NEWS
EARLY EDITION   50¢

Only you are in charge of your destiny!

THE BAD NEWS
LATE EDITION   50¢

Only you are in charge of your destiny!

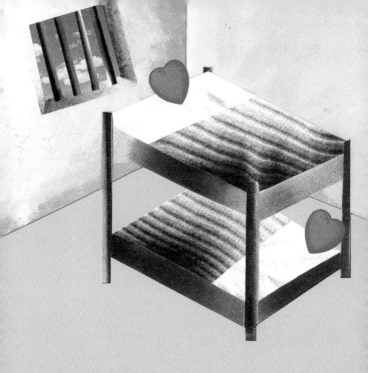

Hold out for a **soulmate**. Don't settle for a **cellmate**.

9 to 5 to 6 to 7 to 8 to

Working mother.
Isn't that redundant?

Sticktoitiveness is brave... but sometimes it's even braver to

unstick yourself from a situation.

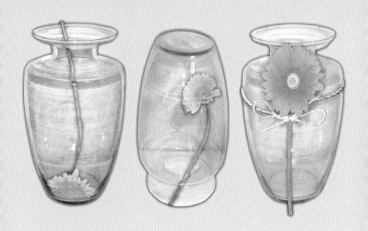

I know I'm making **progress**
because I'm making **new** mistakes.

I'd rather be a role model than a supermodel

The **world** is your oyster...

but you have to have **muscle** to get what you want.

Don't forget not to call

_____

(name of offending jerk here)

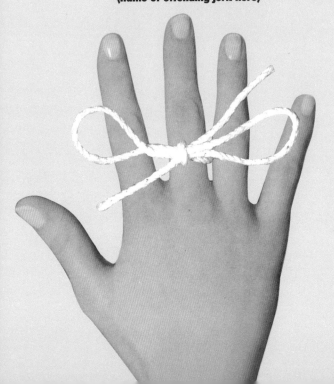

We have to **learn** how to **love** like we learn how to drive. Eventually it all becomes **instinct**.

Stop testing the diving board.

JUM P.

FAST DOESN'T ALWAYS LAST.

FAST DOESN'T ALWAYS LAST.

FAST DOESN'T

ALWAYS LAST.

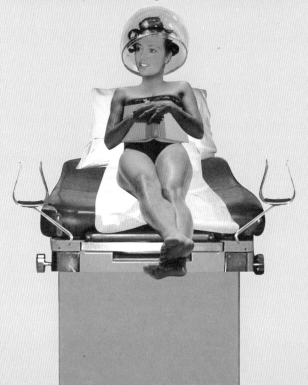

In a **perfect world** . . . gynecologists' offices, hairdressers, and waxing salons would merge.

S.O.R.R.Y.

It's better to be **wrong** some of the time,
than **very right** and **very alone**.

There's only one letter difference between

yet

and

yes.

To get where you need to go
you must first see **who you really are.**

Why is it always

!

(That's ewe I'm talking about.)

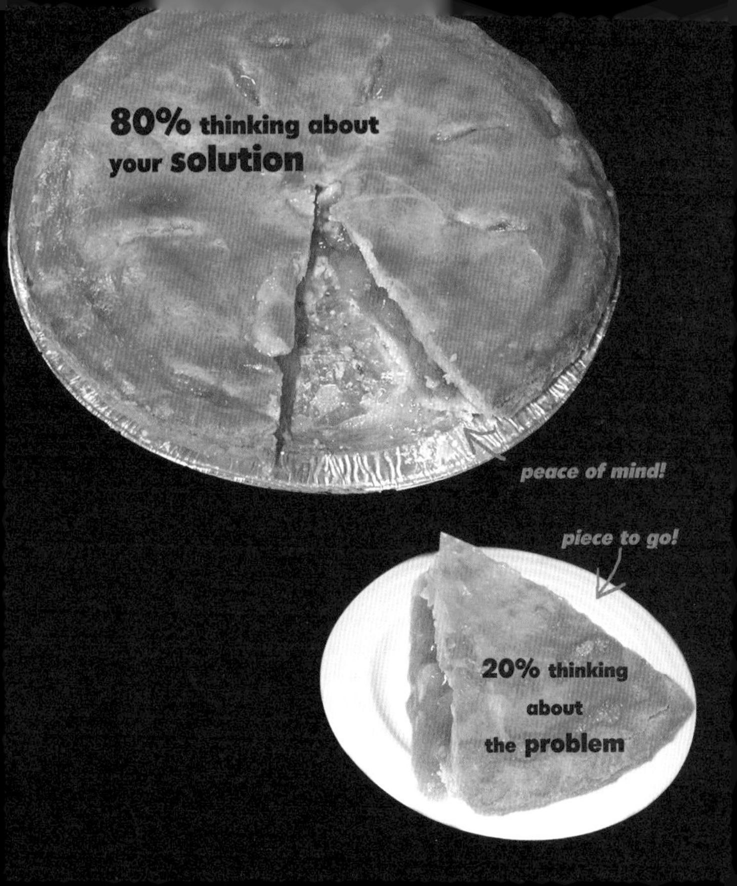
80% thinking about your solution
peace of mind!
piece to go!
20% thinking about the problem

**The quality
of your
communication
EQUALS
the quality
of your
life.**

YOU MUST NOT ONLY
KEEP ON LEARNING...
BUT UN-LEARNING.

This is a world of

yin yang

bad

good

decaf

caffeinated

Transform *regret* into get, get.

Is my ladder against the **right wall?**

Surly to **bed**, surly to **rise.**
Tonight, decide not to go to bed
angry at anyone or anything
that **pissed you off** today.

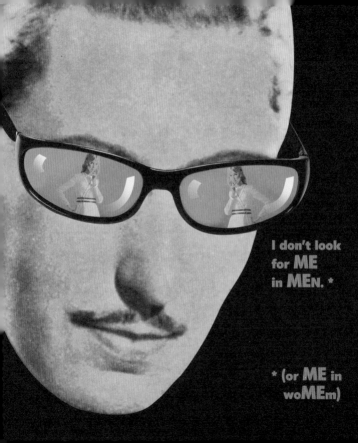

I don't look
for **ME**
in **ME**n. *

* (or **ME** in
wo**ME**m)

The **grass** is always greener on the other side
until you get there and see it's **astrotuf**.

Be

grateful

not

hateful.

Be a **winner** not a **whiner.**

I HATE
MY JOB
4, 1995, 1996, 1997, 1998, 1999, 2000, 20
PRODUCT OF INERTIA

When was the last time you were out?

Be a member of the
fresh air fun.

JUST FOR TODAY:

don't think about it!

I follow the
fuscia brick road.

Size does matter.
Find a guy with a
really big heart.

Forgive
+
Forget

 comes when you

hear with each other's

and see through an other's

I create
my own
good luck.

Saying difficult things now is better than fixing difficult problems later.

It's **better**
to have a
short, bad
relationship
than a
long, bad
relationship.

When you **grow**
you often **outgrow.**

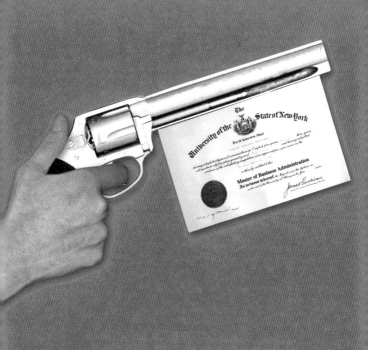

Behind every successful woman is someone who pissed her off.

Love is a **boomerang**.
What you have and **give away**
is what you **get back**.

Be a
WARRIOR
not a
worrier.

I am committed to staying committed to my commitments.
I am committed to staying committed to my commitments.
I am committed to staying committed to my commitments.
I am committed to staying committed to my commitments.
I am committed to staying committed to my commitments.
I am committed to staying committed to my commitments.
I am committed to staying committed to my commitments.
I am committed to staying committed to my commitments.
I am committed to staying committed to my commitments.
I am committed to staying committed to my commitments.
I am committed to staying committed to my commitments.
I am committed to staying committed to my commitments.
I am committed to staying committed to my commitments.
I am committed to staying committed to my commitments.
I am committed to staying committed to my commitments.
I am committed to staying committed to my commitments.
I am committed to staying committed to my commitments.
I am committed to staying committed to my commitments.
I am committed to staying committed to my commitments.
I am committed to staying committed to my commitments.
I am committed to staying committed to my commitments.
I am committed to staying committed to my commitments.
I am committed to staying committed to my commitments.

LOVE IS A TWO-WAY STREET NOT A ROLLER COASTER RIDE

If you want your love life to **be smoking,**
you've got to **stop smoking.**

I have to let myself know what I know, you know?

Sometimes a "NO" is just a slow

YESSSSS

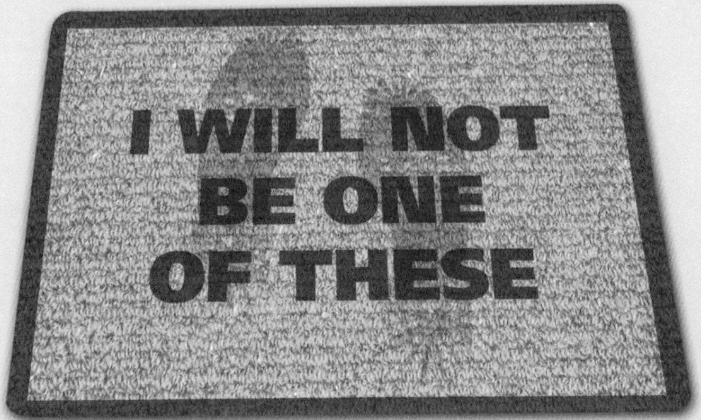
I WILL NOT
BE ONE
OF THESE

DON'T CENSOR YOUR SENSES

See problems

as stepping stones...

not stumbling blocks.

~~Presistance~~

~~Pesistance~~

~~Presistence~~

Persistance is way more important than perfection.

Love **me**, love my **neuroses.**

he loves me

dosen't he?

he loves me

why hasn't he called?

A **pack of puppies**
led by a pit bull
will always be feared
more...

than a **pack
of pit bulls**
led by
a puppy.

Make sure your
burning desire
is the light at the
end of the tunnel.

You've got **sex a-peel.**

Don't let your **convictions** become your **restrictions**.

**NEVER
UH-UH
NO WAY**

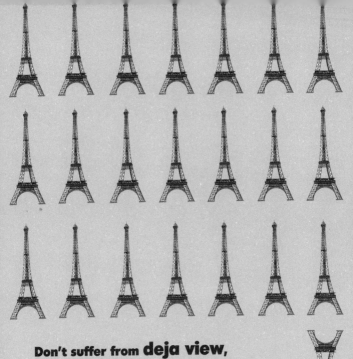

Don't suffer from **deja view**,
always **seeing** things from the
same ol' perspective.

Money doesn't bring happiness.
But happiness does bring money.

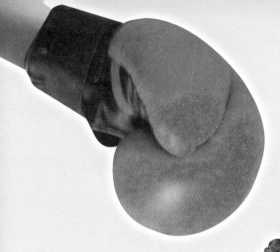

You gotta trust that the universe knows what it's up to when it gives you that **sucker punch.**

A strong enough

WHY

helps you figure out

HOW

Worry is not to be confused with **preparation**.

NOW PLAYING

BASED ON AN UNFORTUNATELY TRUE STORY

My #%?! Life

"A COMEDY" -My Therapist

"A TRAGEDY" -My Mother

"A ROMANTIC HORROR FILM"- My Date

"PG 13 (darnit)"-Yours Truly

What doesn't kill you makes you stronger (and gives you good screenplay material).

Exhasustion is not to be confused with **calm.**

I used to be a **control freak,**
but now **I'm** in control of
being **in control.**

The ability to compromise

is a

very sexy

attribute in a mate.

Bad thoughts always
grow bad circumstances.

 **Birds gotta fly.**

 **Fish gotta swim.**

 **Bitches gotta bitch.**

I gotta _____ .

(Ewe animal, ewe!)

You must be ready to **sweat a lot** to **get a lot.**

All work and **no play** makes Jill reach for the Prozac.

Meditation works like **medication.**
So . . . once a day, rest your mind.

Go get 'em tiger!